Finding Myself ... Am I Enough?

SHEVONICA M HOWELL

ZAKARRI T. CANNON

To order additional copies of this book, contact:
Xlibris
844-714-8691
www.Xlibris.com
Orders@Xlibris.com

ISBN: Softcover   978-1-6641-6746-9
        Hardcover   978-1-6641-6745-2
        EBook   978-1-6641-6747-6

Print information available on the last page

Rev. date: 04/09/2021

Contents

Finding Myself ...Am I Enough?

Shevonica M. Howell

finding myself ... am I enough?

THIS BOOK IS DEDICATED TO THOSE

THAT DON'T HAVE A VOICE, TO THOSE THAT DO AND

TO THOSE THAT FIND IT EASIER TO "JUST" REMAIN SILENT.

WE ARE ALL ENOUGH & I PRAY THAT ONE DAY ... WE WILL ALL

SIMPLY LOVE EACH OTHER FOR THE SKIN WE ARE IN.

fact check:

ACCORDING TO ARTICLES WRITTEN FOR KIDS HEALTH FROM NEMOURS (KIDSHEALTH.ORG), JOHN HOPKINS MEDICINE (HOPKINSMEDICINE.ORG), AND THE NATIONAL INSTITUTE OF NEUROLOGICAL DISORDERS AND STROKES (NINDS) THE FOLLOWING STATEMENTS ARE TRUE:

1. HYDROCEPHALUS IS A CONDITION CHARACTERIZED BY AN ABNORMAL ACCUMULATION OF CEREBROSPINAL FLUID (CSF) WITHIN THE VENTRICLES OF THE BRAIN.

2. THE NATIONAL INSTITUTE OF NEUROLOGICAL DISORDERS AND STROKE (NINDS) ESTIMATES THAT 1 TO 2 OF EVERY 1,000 BABIES ARE BORN WITH HYDROCEPHALUS, HYDROCEPHALUS DOES NOT GO AWAY ON ITS OWN AND NEEDS SPECIAL TREAT.

3. A SHUNT IS A HOLLOW TUBE SURGICALLY PLACED IN THE BRAIN (OR OCCASIONALLY IN THE SPINE) TO HELP DRAIN CEREBROSPINAL FLUID AND REDIRECT IT TO ANOTHER LOCATION IN THE BODY WHERE IT CAN BE REABSORBED.

4. REGULAR, ONGOING CHECKUPS WITH A NEUROSURGEON ARE NECESSARY TO ENJOY A NORMAL LIFE WHEN LIVING WITH A SHUNT.

5. IT IS DIFFICULT TO PREDICT HOW LONG SHUNTS WILL LAST AND [IT IS TRUE] THAT ABOUT A HALF OF ALL SHUNTS MUST BE REVISED OR REPLACED AFTER SIX YEARS.

Zakarri Tashon Cannon

ZAKARRI TASHON CANNON IS A 26-YEAR OLD WHOSE PARENTS RECEIVED NEWS FROM DOCTORS THE DAY SHE WAS BORN THAT CHANGED ALL OF THEIR LIVES AT THAT VERY MOMENT. ZAKARRI'S LIFE STARTED AT 23 WEEKS OF A "SUPPOSEDLY" 36 TO 40 WEEK PROCESS AND TO TOP IT OFF ... SHE WEIGHED IN AT ONLY 1LB 10 OUNCES (SOAK & WET).

THE GOSPEL WAS ...
ZAKARRI WOULDN'T MAKE IT, AND IF SHE DID,
SHE WOULD HAVE SEVERE HEALTH
PROBLEMS HER WHOLE LIFE!

The Start of Continuous Testimonies ☺

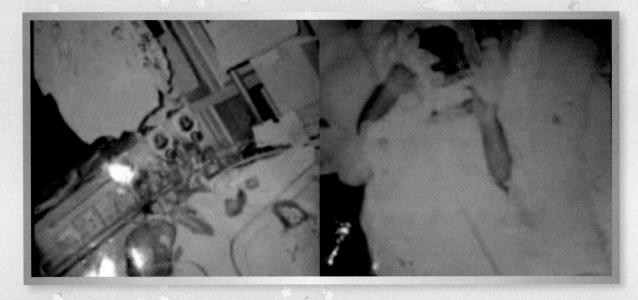

ZAKARRI WAS NOT RELEASED FROM THE HOSPITAL UNTIL AUGUST OF 1995, EXACTLY THREE MONTHS AFTER BEING BORN, DUE TO COMPLICATIONS DURING BIRTH. SHE RECEIVED A VP SHUNT, WAS PLACED ON A HEART MONITOR, AND SLEPT IN AN INCUBATOR UNTIL SHE WAS CLEARED TO GO HOME.

AFTER ZAKARRI'S RELEASE FROM THE HOSPITAL AT THREE MONTHS OLD, SHE BECAME A FREQUENT PATIENT AT HOSPITALS AND CLINICS UNTIL SHE WAS 24-MONTHS OLD. ZAKARRI ENDURED ROUTINE VISITS TO VARIOUS MEDICAL FACILITIES ONCE OR TWICE EVERY WEEK UNTIL SHE WAS PLACED IN THE CARE OF THE EASTER SEALS.

THE EASTER SEALS' NURSES WERE COMPASSIONATE, CARING AND A TRUE BLESSING TO ZAKARRI AND HER FAMILY. THE NURTURING DEMEANORS AND HELPFUL ASSISTANCE GIVEN BY THE NURSES DECREASED THE DAILY STRESS FOR ZAKARRI'S FAMILY...THEY WERE TRULY HEAVEN-SENT.

Interesting Fact:

THE EASTER SEALS IS AN AMERICAN 501(C)(3) NONPROFIT THAT WAS FOUNDED IN 1919. THE NONPROFIT PROVIDES DISABILITY SERVICES, EDUCATION, OUTREACH, AND ADVOCACY SO PEOPLE WITH DISABILITIES CAN LIVE, LEARN, WORK AND PLAY.

Unique Facts About Zakarri:

NAME:

ZAKARRI TASHON CANNON

NICKNAME:

"KAKA"

BIRTH PLACE:

(SHANDS HOSPITAL)

ZODIAC SIGN: TAURUS

ZAKARRI IS THE ELDEST SISTER TO HER SIBLINGS

Family Tree

ZAKARRI TASHON CANNON WAS BORN IN JACKSONVILLE, FLORIDA, ON THURSDAY, MAY 4, 1995. HER MOTHER IS ZENOBIA WHITLEY AND HER LATE FATHER WAS JOSEPH CANNON. ZAKARRI HAS FIVE BROTHERS AND TWO SISTERS.

BIG FACTS:

ZAKARRI LOVES HER FAMILY

Fun Fact:

ZAKARRI'S #1 FAN, HER BEAUTIFUL MOTHER!

THE APPLE DID NOT FALL TO FAR ... FASHIONISTAS

Zakarri & Her Mom

Red Letter Day

ZAKARRI COINED THE TITLE OF THIS CHAPTER IN MEMORY OF HER FATHER, JOSEPH L. CANNON. THE DAY HER FATHER DIED IS A DAY SHE WILL NEVER FORGET. AT 12-YEARS OLD, HAVING TO EXPERIENCE THE DEATH AND BURIAL OF HER DAD FELT LIKE A PART OF HER WAS BURIED THAT DAY. ZAKARRI CAN ONLY RECALL JUST HOW MUCH HER DAD MEANT TO HER AND THE UNCONDITIONAL LOVE HER DAD ALWAYS SHOWED HER. UNDERSTANDING LIFE CHANGES, ZAKARRI CHOOSES TO CARRY ONLY LOVE, MEMORIES AND PEACE IN HER HEART WHEN HER DAD IS CONCERNED. SHE BELIEVES WITHOUT A SHADOW OF DOUBT THAT THEY WILL INDEED MEET AGAIN.

AN UNFORGETTABLE MEMORY:

LOVED BY MANY

MR. JOSEPH L. CANNON PASSED AWAY IN NOVEMBER OF 2007

HE WAS A FATHER & A TRUE FRIEND

(GONE BUT NEVER FORGOTTEN)

Life in Duval

YES, ZAKARRI WAS FAMILIAR WITH HAVING TO VISIT THE HOSPITAL AT LEAST ONCE A MONTH FROM AGE FOUR TO NINE, AND AT LEAST ONCE A YEAR FROM AGE NINE UNTIL PRESENT DUE TO COMPLICATIONS ASSOCIATED WITH HER VP SHUNT, BUT SHE WAS ALSO OBLIGATED TO ENDURE IT! NEEDLESS TO SAY, SHE WAS FOCUSED ON BEING A MOTIVATION TO US ALL!

ZAKARRI CONTINUES TO SHOWER OTHERS WITH LOVE BY WAY OF JUST A SIMPLE TEXT SAYING THAT YOU ARE THOUGHT OF TO GIVING HER MILLION BIRTHDAY SHOUT OUTS TO HER FAVORITE COUSINS TO RANDOM FOLK THAT SHE HAS COME ACROSS THROUGHOUT THE YEARS.

ZAKARRI'S TESTIMONY OF HAVING TO KEEP PUSHING AND NOT GIVING UP WHILE ALSO DEALING WITH MULTIPLE HOSPITAL STAYS THROUGHOUT HER LIFE AS WELL AS ENDURING THE EMOTIONS FELT WHEN HER INITIAL VP SHUNT WAS REVISED IS ... PRICELESS!

Candles Burning on Both Ends

EARLY IN LIFE, ZAKARRI HAD TO UNDERSTAND THE WORDS, TOUGH SKIN! SHE HAD TO TACKLE THE PHRASE, WEARING YOUR FEELINGS ON YOUR SHOULDERS AND FEELING SORRY FOR HERSELF WAS NULL AND VOID!

UNFORTUNATELY, THE HURTFUL WORDS, FAKE FRIEND DRAMA AND THE "KIDS WILL BE KIDS" ERA MADE IT ON ZAKARRI'S DOORSTEP AS WELL.

THERE WERE TIMES THAT SHE WANTED TO CRY, SCREAM, YELL AND KICK BUT SHE CONTINUED TO FOCUS ON GOD AND THE FOLK AROUND HER THAT PUSHED AND CONTINUE TO PUSH HER DAILY!

ZAKARRI OFTEN SPEAKS ABOUT HER MOTHER'S LOVE FOR HER, THE UNCONDITIONAL LOVE FROM HER GRANDPARENTS, A SPECIAL KIND OF LOVE FROM HER AUNTIE WANDA & UNCLE STANLEY, AND THE UNFORGETTABLE LOVE SHE RECEIVED FROM HER DAD.

ZAKARRI ALSO REMINISCES ABOUT TRUE FRIENDSHIPS AND THE AFFECT THAT THOSE FRIENDSHIPS HAVE HAD ON HER ... SHE RECALLS THAT THOSE FRIENDSHIPS ALONG WITH THE GENUINE LOVE THAT HER FAMILY & FRIENDS PROVIDES/PROVIDED HER WITH TRUMPS ANY NEGATIVE THAT SHE EVER CAME INTO CONTACT WITH ...

SPECIAL SHOUT OUTS TO HER TRUE FRIENDS:

CHRISTIAN ALLEN FLANDERS

JARVIS MARQUIS GADSON

RASHARD ISIAH SINGLETARY

 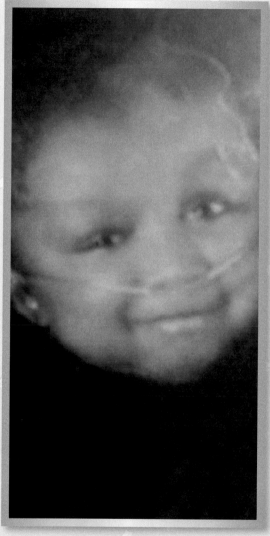

(LEFT) ZAKARRI & HER BEST FRIEND, RASHARD, AT THE
CROWNING OF THE NORTH FLORIDA SCHOOL OF SPECIAL
EDUCATION (RIGHT) JARVIS GADSON, A TRUE FRIEND

RASHARD & JARVIS ARE DEARLY MISSED

School Days

ZAKARRI ATTENDED BILTMORE ELEMENTARY SCHOOL FROM (K-4), NORWOOD ELEMENTARY IN (5TH), KIRBY SMITH MIDDLE IN (6TH), NORTH FLORIDA EDUCATIONAL INSTITUTE FROM (7TH – 11TH), TEMPLE CHRISTIAN ACADEMY FOR A FEW MONTHS DURING (12TH), AND SHE COMPLETED HER REMAINING HIGH SCHOOL YEARS AT NORTH FLORIDA SCHOOL OF SPECIAL EDUCATION. ZAKARRI GRADUATED IN 2017 AT 22-YEARS OLD.

FUN MEMORIES:

THE 2017 HAWAIIAN DANCE

ZAKARRI & CHRISTIAN

ZAKARRI & MRS. ANN ATKINS

all smiles ☺

(LEFT) ZAKARRI'S DATE FOR THE NIGHT TO SHINE PROM AT THE VETERAN MEMORIAL BUILDING, JAMAL KYSER (2018)

(RIGHT) ZAKARRI ENJOYING THE FESTIVITIES WITH MS. ATKINS, BRIANNA NADEAU & SARABETH MCMONEAGLE AT THE

HOLLYWOOD PREMIERE PROM (2016)

ZAKARRI WAS ALWAYS AN ACTIVE STUDENT THAT HAD THE WILL POWER TO WANT TO BE MORE THAN "THE DISABLED GIRL WITH A LIMP & WALKS WITH A WALKER FROM TIME TO TIME."

AS YOU CAN SEE, ZAKARRI WAS ALL SMILES ON GRADUATION NIGHT!

The Big Wave

ZAKARRI COULD REMEMBER WANTING TO SHOW THE NAYSAYERS THAT SHE WAS ENOUGH BY SETTING GOALS THAT MANY FELT WOULD ONLY BE MERE WISHES...RESOLUTIONS IF YOU WILL.

HER TO DO LIST WOULD SEEM MINUTE TO MAYBE A COLLEGE GRADUATE OR EVEN A PERSON DELIVERED FROM A TRADITIONAL CHILDBIRTH (WITH NO SIDE-EFFECTS).

ANYWHO, HER TO DO LIST OR SHOULD I SAY; BUCKET LIST CONSISTED OF THE FOLLOWING:

- GRADUATING FROM HIGH SCHOOL
- BECOMING AN EDUCATOR
- WRITING A BOOK ABOUT HER LIFE/HER STRUGGLES
- HAVING A PLATFORM TO MOTIVATE OTHERS TO NOT GIVE UP

√ ZAKARRI GRADUATED FROM HIGH SCHOOL IN 2017

√ IN JUNE OF 2017, ZAKARRI BECAME A TEACHER'S ASSISTANT AT ACADEMY OF SCHOLARS, INC.

√ THIS IS ZAKARRI'S FIRST PUBLISHED BIOGRAPHY

√ ZAKARRI WILL BE SPEAKING AT HER VERY FIRST BOOK SIGNING ANY DAY NOW

Pretty in Pink

Zakarri's Favorites

FAVORITE COLOR: PINK

FAVORITE SONG: YOU KNOW MY NAME BY TASHA COBB

FAVORITE BIBLE VERSE: JEREMIAH 29:13

FAVORITE RESTAURANT: RED LOBSTERS

FAVORITE FOOD: SHRIMP ALFREDO

FAVORITE BOOK: GIRL, THEY AIN'T READY!

FAVORITE HOBBY: READING

Zakarri Tashon Cannon is More Than Enough

Factual synopsis:

ZAKARRI TASHON CANNON IS ALL THAT AND

"THREE" BAGS OF CHIPS!

"LETTING HER HATERS BE HER MOTIVATOR"

Glossary

GRATEFUL- FEELING OR SHOWING AN APPRECIATION OF KINDNESS; THANKFUL.

COPING – TO DEAL WITH AND ATTEMPT TO OVERCOME PROBLEMS AND DIFFICULTIES.

ENOUGH – IN OR TO A DEGREE OR QUANTITY THAT SATISFIES.

LOVED - TO FEEL A DEEP AFFECTION FOR (SOMEONE); TO LIKE OR ENJOY VERY MUCH.

HOPE – A FEELING OF EXPECTATION AND DESIRE FOR A CERTAIN THING TO HAPPEN.

FAITH – COMPLETE TRUST OR CONFIDENCE IN SOMEONE OR SOMETHING.

DEPRESSION – A MENTAL HEALTH DISORDER THAT CAUSES FEELINGS OF SADNESS AND/OR LOSS OF INTEREST.

LONELY - SAD BECAUSE ONE HAS NO FRIENDS OR COMPANY.

STRENGTH – THE QUALITY OR STATE OF BEING STRONG,

DETERMINATION – FIRMNESS OF PURPOSE; RESOLUTENESS.

DISABILITY – ANY CONDITION OF THE BODY OR MIND (IMPAIRMENT) THAT MAKES IT MORE DIFFICULT FOR THE PERSON WITH THE CONDITION TO DO CERTAIN ACTIVITIES (ACTIVITY LIMITATIONS) AND INTERACT WITH THE WORLD AROUND THEM.

CARE – TO FEEL CONCERN OR INTEREST; ATTACH IMPORTANCE TO SOMETHING.

FAMILY – A GROUP OF ONE OR MORE PARENTS AND THEIR CHILDREN LIVING TOGETHER AS A UNIT.

Spelling Assignment

DIRECTIONS: UNSCRAMBLE THE FOLLOWING WORDS FROM THE GLOSSARY.

1. A I S D I L Y B T I _____

2. L E D V O _____

3. S G T R E T N H _____

4. G O E U H N _____

5. S E P S N R E I D O _____

6. G F T L E A R U _____

7. L Y N E O L _____

8. T F I A H _____

9. P O E H _____

10. I O C P N G _____

11. R C E A _____

12. F Y M L I A _____

Book Review

1. WHO WAS THIS BOOK ABOUT? _____

2. WHEN WAS HE OR SHE BORN? _____

3. COULD YOU RELATE TO HIS OR HER CHALLENGES? _____

4. IF YOU COULD RELATE TO HIS OR HER CHALLENGES, EXPLAIN.

_____

_____

5. WHO IS THE AUTHOR OF THIS BOOK? _____

6. WHY DO YOU THINK THIS BOOK WAS WRITTEN? _____
_____

7. WHAT DID YOU LIKE ABOUT THIS BOOK? _____
_____

8. WHAT WOULD YOUR BOOK BE ABOUT AND WHAT WOULD YOU NAME IT?

_____

_____

_____

9. IF YOU COULD MEET THE CHARACTER OF THIS BOOK, WHAT WOULD YOU SAY TO KEEP HIM OR HER MOTIVATED TO NOT GIVE UP?

_____

_____

10. WHO IS YOUR MENTOR AND/OR ROLE MODEL? _____

_____

11. LIST TWO THINGS THAT YOU LIKE ABOUT THE BOOK AND TWO THINGS THAT YOU DISLIKE.

_____

_____

_____

_____

Reading Assignment

USE THE WORDS FROM THE GLOSSARY TO ANSWER THE FOLLOWING QUESTIONS.

1. DEFINE DISABILITY. _____

_____

_____

2. A FEELING OF EXPECTATION AND DESIRE FOR A CERTAIN THING TO

HAPPEN IS CALLED _____

3. THE QUALITY OR STATE OF BEING STRONG IS CALLED _____

_____

4. COPING MEANS TO DEAL WITH AND ATTEMPT TO OVERCOME PROBLEMS AND DIFFICULTIES. TRUE OR FALSE _____

5. LONELY MEANS TO BE HAPPY BECAUSE ONE HAS MANY FRIENDS OR COMPANY. TRUE/FALSE _____

6. GRATEFUL IS AN ACT OF SHOWING A FEELING OR SHOWING AN

_____ OF KINDNESS; THANKFUL.

7. TO BE LOVED MEANS TO FEEL A DEEP _____

FOR (SOMEONE); TO LIKE OR ENJOY VERY MUCH.

8. DEFINE DETERMINATION._____

_____

_____

9. IN YOUR OWN WORDS, DEFINE DISABILITY _____

_____

_____

Word Search Puzzle

GRATEFUL	COPING	ENOUGH	CARE
LOVED	HOPE	FAITH	FAMILY
LONELY	STRENGTH	DISABILITY	DEPRESSION

C	Z	G	N	I	P	O	C	U	B
E	N	O	U	G	H	A	R	E	L
H	T	G	N	E	R	T	S	P	O
D	E	P	R	E	S	S	I	O	N
F	A	M	I	L	Y	J	M	H	E
G	R	A	T	E	F	U	L	X	L
D	I	S	A	B	I	L	I	T	Y
F	A	I	T	H	D	E	V	O	L

To: Zakarri

FROM: Ms. Howell

IT WAS TRULY AN HONOR TO WRITE ABOUT A YOUNG WOMAN THAT CONTINUES TO SMILE, SHOW KINDNESS, LOVE UNCONDITIONALLY AND MAKE HER HATERS HER MOTIVATOR! SHE IS GOD-FEARING AND HER LOVE FOR OTHERS IS PURE. SHE HAS OFTEN ASKED HER GOD IF SHE IS ENOUGH AND ALTHOUGH I AM NOT, HE! I AM ECSTATIC TO SAY THAT SHE IS MORE THAN ENOUGH AND FROM THE WORDS OF MAYA ANGELO, "CAUSE [SHE IS] A WOMAN PHENOMENALLY. PHENOMENAL WOMAN, [IS SHE]."

More books related to this title:

GIRL, THEY AIN'T READY! (2011)

I CAN DIG IT SIS ... THEY AIN'T READY! (2017)

WHAT'S IN A NAME? (2018)

A PLAY WITH WORDS WORD SEARCH BOOK (2020)

THE 'YOU TEACH IT" MATH STUDY GUIDE (2020)

WE LOVE YOU, DRE! (2021)

A IS FOR AUDRE' (2021)

TE'RANA ALIYAH ... A BEAUTY WITH BRAINS (2021)

Printed in the United States
by Baker & Taylor Publisher Services